IOWA Assessment Practice Workbook (Grade 1)

Table Of Contents

Math - Section 1

Today you will be taking IOWA Assessment. You will hear each question only once. Try to answer all the questions. If you are not sure of the answer, choose the one you think is best.

Sample Question: Which word says how many cars there are?

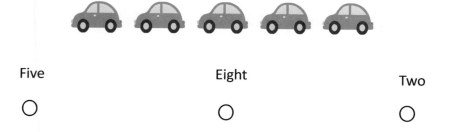

Five

Eight

Two

○   ○   ○

Q1. Which group has one carrot for each bunny with none left over? Select the group of carrots that shows one carrot for each bunny with none left over.

○   ○   ○

Q2. Which doghouse has an entrance shaped like a pentagon? Select the doghouse with the entrance shaped like a pentagon.

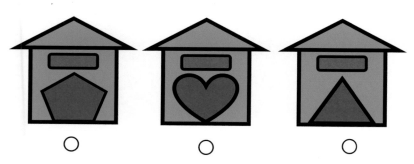

○   ○   ○

Q3. Samantha's school was collecting quarters to buy a new swing. Each class had a container to collect quarters. Fill the circle under the picture that can contain the most quarters.

    ○   ○   ○

Q4. Which symbol should go in the box to make the number sentence true? Select the symbol that makes the number sentence true.

8   ?   4 = 12

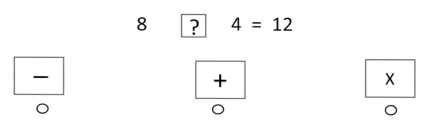

    ○   ○   ○

Q5. Cats below follow a pattern. Select the cat that goes next in the pattern.

    ○   ○   ○

Q6. Lila has a big sister. Lila wants to know how tall her sister is. Which one Lila should use to find out how tall her sister is?

    ○   ○   ○

Q7. Hailey and her sister mow the lawns for their neighbors. They get paid 6 dollars for each lawn they mow. Which number sentence can Hailey use to find out how much will they earn if they mow four lawns?

    4+4+4+4=16   6+6+4+4=20   4 X 6 = 24

        ○   ○   ○

Q8. How much is 2 dimes and 4 nickels? Select the amount that is same as 2 dimes and 4 nickels.

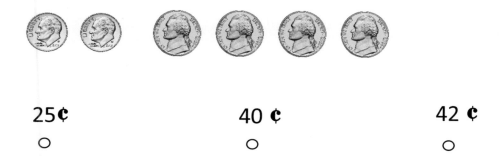

    25¢   40 ¢   42 ¢

    ○   ○   ○

Q9. Which horse is 4th from the right? Fill in the circle under the 4th horse from the right.

    ○   ○   ○

Q10. Which number should go in the box to make the number sentence true? Select the number that makes the number sentence true.

$$6 + \boxed{} = 13$$

5
◯

7
◯

6
◯

Q11. Which subtraction fact tells about the picture? Select the subtraction fact that tells about the picture.

5 − 4 = 1
◯

5 − 1 = 4
◯

4 − 1 = 3
◯

Q12. How much is 5 tens and 9 ones? Select the picture which is same as 5 tens and 9 ones.

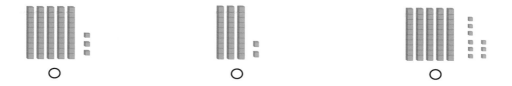

◯   ◯   ◯

Q13. Which of these shows a line of symmetry? Select the picture that shows a line of symmetry.

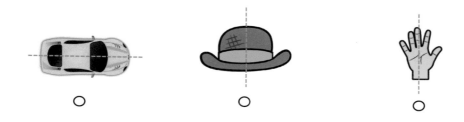

◯   ◯   ◯

Q14. One duck is missing a number to complete the pattern.
Select the number that is missing.

13   10   12
○   ○   ○

Q15. Samantha's mom bought juice for Samantha's birthday party.
Which unit of measure is best for how much juice she bought?

kilogram   meters   liters
○   ○   ○

Q16. Which picture is one - fourth shaded? Select the picture that is
one - fourth shaded.

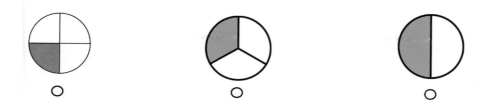

○   ○   ○

Q17. Which present is shaped like a cylinder?

○   ○   ○

Q18. Susan's school starts at 8:45. Which clock shows 8:45am?

○   ○   ○

Q19. Naomi's mom gave her 14 dollars to spend at the school fair. She spent 6 dollars on the rides and saved the rest. Which number sentence shows how much money she saved? Select the number sentence that shows how much money Naomi saved?

14 - 6 = 7   14 - 6 = 8   8 + 6 = 14
○   ○   ○

Q20. Which number is about 60? Select the number that is about 60.

53   51   56
○   ○   ○

Q21. Which number makes the number sentence true? Select the number that makes the number sentence true.

$$17 - \boxed{?} = 11$$

3   9   6
○   ○   ○

Q22. The pictures show a bicycle, pencil and bed. Which one weighs about 50 pounds in real life? Fill the circle under picture that weighs 50 pounds in real life.

O   O   O

Q23. These are the scores of three tests that Lola took. Which is the lowest score? Select the lowest score.

68   56   93
O   O   O

Q24. How much is 3 Nickels and 2 pennies?

32   17   25
O   O   O

Q25. Darbie's friends visited the zoo. The ticket cost 45 cents. Which picture shows 45 cents? Select the picture that shows exactly 45 cents.

O   O   O

Q26. Kelly used 5 boxes of chocolates for her birthday party. Each box had 4 chocolates. Which number sentence Kelly can use to find out how many chocolates were there in all. Select the number sentence Kelly can use to find out the how many chocolates there were in all?

5 X 4 = 20   4 X 4 = 16   5 + 4 = 9

○   ○   ○

Math - Section 2

Today you will be taking IOWA Assessment. You will hear each question only once. Try to answer all the questions. If you are not sure of the answer, choose the one you think is best.

Use the circle graph to answer questions 1 and 2

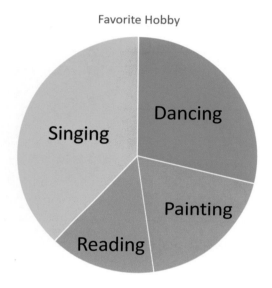

Favorite Hobby

Q1. Which of these hobbies got fewer votes than dancing did?

Singing and Reading   Reading and Painting   Gymnastics and Singing

◯   ◯   ◯

Q2. Which of these hobbies got the most votes?

Singing   Swimming   Dancing

◯   ◯   ◯

One day Tabitha's class voted for their favorite pet. The graph shows how many kids like dogs, cat, bunny, fish and frogs. Each picture stands for 1 kid. Use the picture graph to answer questions 3 to 6.

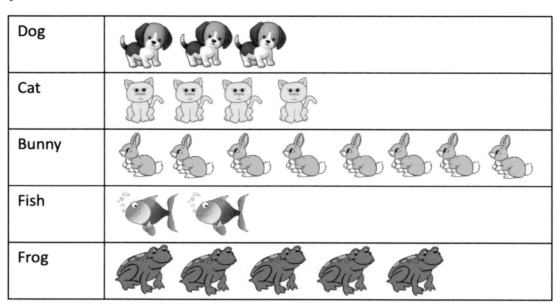

Q3. Which pet got the fewest votes?

Bunny	Frog	Fish
○	○	○

Q4. The number of kids that voted for frog was same as the number of kids that voted for which two animals together

Dog and Fish	Dog and cat	Frog and Fish
○	○	○

Q5. Twice as many kids voted bunny as one other animal.

Dog	Cat	Fish
○	○	○

One day students in Grade 3 and 4 voted for their favorite dessert. The table shows how many children in each grade like cupcake, donut, ice cream and candy. Listen to the question and then choose the best answer.

	3rd Grade	4th Grade
Cupcake	3	4
Donut	4	6
Ice Cream	3	5
Candy	1	2

Q6. Which dessert was picked by fewer than four kids in grade 4?

donut   candy   cupcake
  ○   ○   ○

Q7. Which two desserts were picked by the same number of grade 3 students?

cupcake and ice cream   candy   cupcake
      ○   ○   ○

Q8. Which dessert was picked by fewer than 3 children in grade 3?

candy   cupcake   donut
  ○   ○   ○

Q9. How many grade 3 and grade 4 children voted in all?

25   32   28

○   ○   ○

Now you will do another kind of question. This is a test of math problem solving. You will hear some problem. You have to work on the problem. When you have decided on an answer look at the three numbers, if your answer is there, fill the circle under it. If your answer is not there then fill the circle under "N". Which stands for not given. You will hear each problem twice.

Sample 1: Sarah bought five dolls. She already had three dolls. How many dolls Sarah has in all?

9   8   10   N

○   ○   ○   ○

Sample 2: At the Zoo Natlie saw 4 lions and 7 hippos. How many lions and hippos in all did she see?

12   10   15   N

○   ○   ○   ○

Q10: Hazel collects dolls. She started with 6 and got 4 more. How many dolls does Hazel have in all?

10	11	9	N
○	○	○	○

Q11: Noah and some friends went on a beach. Noah found 5 seashells; his friend David found 8 seashells, but his friend Scott did not find any. How many shells did the boys find in all?

12	10	15	N
○	○	○	○

Q12: Arianna made 4 cards for her family. For each card she used 2 colored papers. Every color was different. How many papers did Arianna use in all?

6	7	8	N
○	○	○	○

Q13: Natalie had 8 skirts. 2 were red, 4 were blue and rest were green. How many skirts were green?

2	1	5	N
○	○	○	○

Q14: 5 Students had to divide the box of crayon equally. There were 15 crayons in one box. How many crayons will each student get?

4	3	15	N
○	○	○	○

Q15: Harold got 10 strawberries for snack. He ate 4 strawberries. How many strawberries were left?

6	4	14	N
○	○	○	○

Math - Section 3

Today you will be taking IOWA Assessment. You will hear each question only once. Try to answer all the questions. If you are not sure of the answer, choose the one you think is best.

This is math test. In this section you will hear an addition problem. Choose the best answer. If you don't see the answer, choose "N", which means not given.

Sample 1: What is 2 plus 3? 2 plus 3 equals what number?

4	1	5	N
○	○	○	○

Sample 2: What is 4 plus 1? 4 plus 1 equals what number?

4	7	9	N
○	○	○	○

Q1: What is 8 plus 4? 8 plus 4 is what number?

12	9	11	N
○	○	○	○

Q2: What is 73 plus 4? 73 plus 4 is what number?

76	88	77	N
○	○	○	○

Q3: What is 7 plus 7? 7 plus 7 is what number?

16	14	15	N
○	○	○	○

Q4: What is 15 plus 6? 15 plus 6 is what number?

23	24	14	N
○	○	○	○

Now you will do some subtraction problems

Q5: What is 17 take away 5? 17 minus 5 is what number?

11	12	10	N
○	○	○	○

Q6: What is 14 take away 6? 14 minus 6 is what number?

8	10	7	N
○	○	○	○

Q7: What is 48 take away 3? 48 minus 3 is what number?

46	45	51	N
○	○	○	○

Q8: What is 8 take away 2? 8 minus 2 is what number?

7	4	5	N
○	○	○	○

This section will have both addition and subtraction problems

Q9. 14 + 7 = ?

21	18	17	N
○	○	○	○

Q10: 46 − 5 = ?

40	41	51	N
○	○	○	○

Q11: 12 + 6 = ?

17	18	15	N
○	○	○	○

Q12: 19 − 4 = ?

13	8	15	N
○	○	○	○

Q13. 83 + 4 = ?

21	87	77	N
◯	◯	◯	◯

Q14: 10 − 7 = ?

6	5	1	N
◯	◯	◯	◯

Q15: 29 + 5 = ?

34	32	26	N
◯	◯	◯	◯

Q16: 21 − 2 = ?

23	19	17	N
◯	◯	◯	◯

This is a test about the meaning of words. In each question in this section there is a picture and four words. One of the four words tells about the picture. You must read the four words and decide which one best tells about the picture. Then choose that word.

Sample Question

○ elephant

○ grey

○ tiger

○ jungle

Q1.

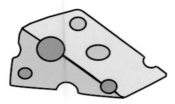

- ○ yellow
- ○ butter
- ○ cheese
- ○ mouse

Q2.

- ○ football
- ○ basketball
- ○ sphere
- ○ basket

Q3.

- ○ cube
- ○ pretty
- ○ gift
- ○ birthday

Q4.

- ○ fingers
- ○ arm
- ○ wrist
- ○ ankle

Q5.

- ○ guitar
- ○ harp
- ○ music
- ○ strings

Q6.

- ○ caterpillar
- ○ tadpole
- ○ worm
- ○ fish

Q7.

- ○ group
- ○ flock
- ○ geese
- ○ school

Q8.

- ○ yacht
- ○ ship
- ○ sailboat
- ○ canoe

Q9.

- ○ Sewing
- ○ knitting
- ○ cloths
- ○ craft

Q10.

- ○ hunt
- ○ swoop
- ○ glide
- ○ float

Q11.

- ○ boat
- ○ swimming
- ○ submarine
- ○ tugboat

Q12.

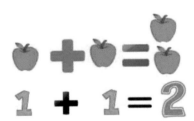

- ○ Subtraction
- ○ division
- ○ problem
- ○ addition

Q13.

- ○ collar
- ○ mane
- ○ hair
- ○ muzzle

Q14.

- ○ hammer
- ○ Screw driver
- ○ nail
- ○ wrench

Q15.

- ○ running
- ○ swimming
- ○ skipping
- ○ dancing

Each of the sentences in this part has a word missing. Under each sentence are four words. You should decide which word belongs in the sentence and choose that word.

Sample Question

Biggest planet in our solar system is _____.

Mars   Venus   Earth   Jupiter
○   ○   ○   ○

Q1: Animals that can live both in the water and land are called _____.

reptile   amphibian   insects   fish

○   ○   ○   ○

Q2: We use a _____, when we are making scrambled eggs.

fork   knife   whisk   plate

○   ○   ○   ○

Q3: _____has eight arms and two tentacles.

squid   octopus   bird   jelly Fish

○   ○   ○   ○

Q4: The rockets _____ engines lifted it into space.

fantastic   powerful   noisy   small

○   ○   ○   ○

Q5: A group of fish is called _____.

flock   fishes   school   litter
○   ○   ○   ○

Q6: Bees suck _____ from the flowers.

bugs   colors   juice   nectar
○   ○   ○   ○

Q7: If koala bears don't eat leaves, they will _____.

starve   glad   sleep   dissatisfied
○   ○   ○   ○

Q8: Many dinosaurs were _____ creatures.

small   gigantic   tiny   little
○   ○   ○   ○

Q9: Pirates look for hidden _____.

gifts ○　　　rocks ○　　　treasures ○　　　yacht ○

Q10: Mia was _____ after her soccer practice.

exhausted ○　　　fresh ○　　　upset ○　　　energized ○

Q11: Foxes are very _____.

sneaky ○　　　gigantic ○　　　slow ○　　　noisy ○

Q12: Lin gets _____ when it's dark.

pleased ○　　　excited ○　　　terrified ○　　　confident ○

This is a reading test. Each question has a picture. Below the picture is a sentence which tells something about the picture. Each sentence has a missing word. You must look at the three words below the sentence that best fits in the sentence.

Q1: There are two _____ on the floor.

blocks   books   balls

◯   ◯   ◯

Q2: There is a _____ on the chest of drawers.

lamp   ball   globe

◯   ◯   ◯

Q3: There is a _____ next to the robot.

truck   soccer ball   slippers

◯   ◯   ◯

Q4: Jena is stacking the _____ on the floor.

blocks   books   balls

○   ○   ○

Q5: There is a _____ on the windowsill.

globe   plant   puppet

○   ○   ○

Q6: Mrs. Chuck is holding a _____ in her hand.

picture   pencil   puppet

○   ○   ○

Q7: Lyla is standing with tooth _____.

mirror   pain   brush

◯   ◯   ◯

Q8: Daniel is getting his teeth _____.

painted   yanked   checked

◯   ◯   ◯

Q9: Dr. Wang is a _____.

engineer   dentist   scientist

◯   ◯   ◯

This is a reading test. Each question in this part has a story. First you should read the story then read the question below the story. There are three answers to each question but only one of the answers is right. Then you will choose the answer you think is best.

Once upon a time, there was a lion named Leo who was the king of the jungle. He had a loud roar and sharp teeth, but he also had a kind heart. One day, he heard a little rabbit crying for help and used his strong paws to dig him out of a hole. The rabbit and Leo became friends, and all the other animals saw that even though Leo was big and strong, he had a kind heart too.

Q1: Who was the king of the jungle?

Rabbit   Leo   Simba
○   ○   ○

Q2: Who did Leo save from the hole?

dear   mouse   rabbit
○   ○   ○

Q3: What did Leo use to dig the rabbit out of the hole?

paws   shovel   teeth
○   ○   ○

Once upon a time, there were two best friends named Lily and Sarah. They did everything together, from playing at the park to sharing their lunch at school. They were inseparable, and their friendship was unbreakable.

One day, Lily moved to a new city, and Sarah was very sad. She missed her friend and didn't know how to make new friends. But Lily and Sarah kept in touch, talking on the phone and writing letters. They even planned a special visit for the summer.

When Lily came to visit, Sarah introduced her to some of her new friends. Lily was happy to see that Sarah had made new friends, but she was still her best friend. And Sarah was happy to see that Lily had made new friends too.

Even though they lived far away from each other, their friendship remained strong. They knew that distance couldn't break the bond they shared.

Q4: Who were the two best friends in the story?

Lily and Tom   Sarah and Lila   Sarah and Lily
   ○   ○   ○

Q5: What did Lily and Sarah do together?

Playing at the park   Swimming at pool   Reading books
   ○   ○   ○

Q6: How did Lily and Sarah stay in touch?

playing together   talking on phone   watching television
   ○   ○   ○

Fishing is a fun activity that many people enjoy. To go fishing, you need a fishing rod, fishing line, and a hook with bait on it. When you cast your line into the water, you wait patiently for a fish to bite. If you feel a tug on your line, that means a fish has taken your bait. Then you have to reel the fish in. When you catch a fish, you can either keep it or release it back into the water.

Fishing can be done in many places such as a lake, river, or even in the ocean. It is important to always be careful around water and to wear a life jacket. Remember to always clean up after yourself and not to leave any trash behind.

Q7: What do you need to go fishing?

fishing rod   fish   boat
   ○   ○   ○

Q8: What does it mean when you feel a tug on your line?

○ fish has taken your bait

○ line got stuck in the water

○ fishing is done

Q9: What should you wear when fishing near water?

boots   jacket   life jacket
   ○   ○   ○

Lily was nervous to go to the dentist. She had never been before, and she was scared that it would hurt. When Lily arrived at the dentist's office, she saw a friendly lady who introduced herself as Dr. Lee.

Dr. Lee asked Lily to open her mouth, and then she looked at her teeth with a little mirror. Lily didn't feel any pain, and Dr. Lee was very gentle.

After the checkup, Dr. Lee gave Lily a sticker for being brave. Lily left the dentist's office feeling proud of herself and happy to have healthy teeth.

Q10: Where was Lily scared to go?

doctor   school   dentist

○   ○   ○

Q11: What did Dr. Lee give Lily for being brave?

toy car   sticker   tooth brush

○   ○   ○

Answer Key

Math Section 1

1. C
2. A
3. C
4. B
5. A
6. C
7. C
8. B
9. C
10. B
11. B
12. C
13. A
14. C
15. C
16. A
17. B
18. C
19. B
20. C
21. C
22. C
23. B
24. B
25. A
26. A

Math Section 2

1. B
2. A
3. C
4. A
5. B
6. B
7. A
8. A
9. C
10. A
11. D
12. C
13. A
14. B
15. A

Math Section 3

1. A
2. C
3. B
4. D
5. B
6. A
7. B
8. D
9. A
10. B
11. B
12. C
13. B
14. D
15. A
16. B

Language Section 1

1. C
2. B
3. C
4. C
5. B
6. B
7. B
8. C
9. A
10. B
11. C
12. D
13. B
14. B
15. C

Language Section 2

1. B
2. C
3. B
4. B
5. C
6. D
7. A
8. B
9. C
10. A
11. A
12. C

Language Section 3

1. C
2. A
3. B
4. A
5. B
6. C
7. B
8. C
9. B

Language Section 4

1. B
2. C
3. A
4. C
5. A
6. B
7. A
8. A
9. C
10. C
11. B

Made in United States
Troutdale, OR
12/20/2023